LOL

A KEEPSAKE JOURNAL OF HILARIOUS Q&As

BRANDON T. SNIDER

STERLING CHILDREN'S BOOKS
New York

STERLING CHILDREN'S BOOKS
New York

An Imprint of Sterling Publishing
1166 Avenue of the Americas
New York, NY 10036

STERLING CHILDREN'S BOOKS and the distinctive Sterling Children's
Books logo are trademarks of Sterling Publishing Co., Inc.

© 2016 by Sterling Publishing Co., Inc.

ISBN 978-1-4549-1833-2

Distributed in Canada by Sterling Publishing
c/o Canadian Manda Group, 664 Annette Street
Toronto, Ontario, Canada M6S 2C8.
Distributed in the United Kingdom by GMC Distribution Services
Castle Place, 166 High Street, Lewes, East Sussex, England BN7 1XU
Distributed in Australia by Capricorn Link (Australia) Pty. Ltd.
P.O. Box 704, Windsor, NSW 2756, Australia

For information about custom editions, special sales, and premium and corporate purchases, please
contact Sterling Special Sales at 800-805-5489 or specialsales@sterlingpublishing.com.

Design by 3&Co.

Manufactured in China
Lot #:
2 4 6 8 10 9 7 5 3 1
01/16

www.sterlingpublishing.com

Hi there!

It's your lucky day. Know why? The journal you're holding in your hands is going to become the funniest thing in the history of the world. FOR REAL. (Maybe!) You'll be asked to write about hilarious things you've experienced as well as weird stuff you MIGHT experience. You'll also be asked to draw stuff and give your opinions about all things hysterical. It's all about finding the humor in life. And here's the catch: NO ONE WILL SEE IT BUT YOU. That means you should feel free and clear to write about whatever you want. Experiment! No judgments. Use this journal to discover your own unique brand of humor. Lots of stuff can be funny under the right set of circumstances. Humor can be light and it can be dark. It can also make you think about life and help work out your problems. (Seriously.) Your goal should be to have as much fun as possible. Make yourself laugh. This is your place to do whatever you want without ANY boundaries. Oh, and humor comes from the truth so make sure you're as honest as you can be. GO WILD.

Now open this thing up and
GET CRACKIN'!

If your life was a **comedic book**,
what would it be called?

What if that book was made into a **comedic movie**?
What would it be called then?

Now, say there was a funny **spin-off TV show**?
What'd that be called?

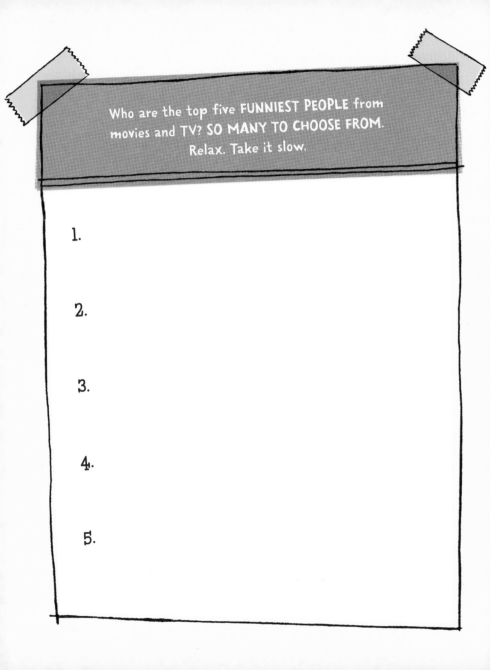

Who are the top five **FUNNIEST PEOPLE** from movies and TV? **SO MANY TO CHOOSE FROM.** Relax. Take it slow.

1.

2.

3.

4.

5.

What is the weirdest and funniest dream you've ever had? Describe what happened in as much detail as possible. It might be hard to remember but try!

Are you in a band? YOU ARE NOW. Draw your band logo.
Make it **hilarious** and awe-inspiring.

Fill in the blanks.

Fill in each blank with the type of word it requires.
Don't read ahead or think too much. Just do it!

I always feel_____ when I've got
                            [adjective]

a/an _____ in my hand. You can do
                 [noun]

so many things with it! You can _____
                                    [verb]

a/an _____. It will help you remove
                 [noun]

_____ _____
    [adjective]   [plural noun]

from an old _____. Just don't
                       [noun]

_____ with it and you'll be fine. It's
       [verb]

so easy that a/an_____can use it!
                        [animal]

What if your mom or dad started doing stand-up comedy? Would it be weird for you? Would you get embarrassed if they shared a lot of personal stuff on stage? Write about how you'd feel.

_____

_____

_____

_____

_____

_____

_____

_____

_____

_____

_____

_____

_____

How do you greet a troll properly? Do you shake hands?
Do you wink and drool? (That would be weird.) Show the world
the proper etiquette in four easy steps.

Write five strange and funny compliments
you might give someone.

1.

2.

3.

4.

5.

Would you rather tell someone you don't know very well that you love them **OR** tell someone you know very well that you don't love them?

Would you rather chew a slug for five minutes **OR** keep a live cricket in your mouth for five minutes?

Would you rather shave your head **OR** wear the ugliest wig in the world for a whole week?

If your family had a **mascot**, what would it be?

_____

If you were an **undercover spy**, what would your

nickname be?

_____

If you had your **own awards show**, what would

it be called?

_____

Write the **first thing** that pops into your brain after each word. Don't think about it.

Doe

Bizarre

Skillet

Basic

Ride

Bunny

Knight

Night

Take a good hard look at your answers on the previous page, and really THINK about them. Do you know why you wrote down the words that you did? Figure out your thought process, and try to justify some of your responses.

_____

_____

_____

_____

_____

_____

_____

_____

_____

_____

_____

_____

There's an old saying that "Life is like a box full of used diapers ... FULL OF IT!" (Actually that one's totally new.) Why not come up with some funny philosophies of your own?

1.

2.

3.

4.

5.

Now select one of your new wisdom-filled phrases from the previous page, and draw an inspirational poster around it. Share your worldly knowledge with us, great one. Show us the way!

Have you ever had something embarrassing happen on social media? Ugh. That's the worst. But I'm sure you learned a good lesson and can laugh about it now, right? Write about the situation and how it made you feel.

Dreams can mean **EVERYTHING**. Or nothing at all. Think about a dream you've had, and analyze it in a funny way. What's it **REALLY** about? It doesn't have to be correct, just have some fun!

Wouldja make a kissy face at a strange old lady? **YES** or **NO**

Wouldja moon someone from really far away? **YES** or **NO**

Wouldja call The Rock a big, fat baby-man? **YES** or **NO**

Wouldja draw a smiley face on a famous painting? **YES** or **NO**

Select your favorite and least favorite question from the previous page. Did you respond **YES** or **NO**? Write about your answers and explain why you would (or wouldn't) do the activity.

_____

_____

_____

_____

_____

_____

_____

_____

_____

_____

What are the top five funniest books you've ever read? (You can't include this journal even though your answers are totally hilarious!)

1.

2.

3.

4.

5.

Leave out a fake diary entry from a fictional person for someone to accidentally find. Keep an eye on the situation, and then report back. What happened? Write about the experience.

Wouldja show off your weirdest swimming moves
in a public pool? **YES** or **NO**

Wouldja sell all of your personal belongings "just cuz"?
YES or **NO**

Wouldja wipe a booger on your friend? **YES** or **NO**

Wouldja blame a fart on your mom? **YES** or **NO**

Select your favorite and least favorite question from the previous page. Did you respond **YES** or **NO**? Write about your answers and explain why you would (or wouldn't) do the activity.

_____

_____

_____

_____

_____

_____

_____

_____

_____

_____

What's the most embarrassing question
you've ever been asked?
What did you answer?

What's the most embarrassing question
you've ever asked someone?
What did they answer?

What's a **funny talent** that you have?

_____

_____

What's a funny talent that a **friend** or

family member has?

_____

_____

What's a funny talent that you **wish you had**?

_____

_____

Wear a shirt inside out for an entire day. Tell people you're celebrating International Topsy Turvy Day. See if you can convince friends to join you, and write about the experience.

Give yourself a wild hairstyle, and wear it around for the day. When people ask, tell them it's the NEW YOU! Watch how people respond, and then write about it.

How do you put lipstick on a shark? Is that even possible?
You've got four panels to show the world how to do it.
It better be funny too. Now get to drawin'!

What's the most awkward question that you hope
no one EVER asks you? Why don't you want to answer?
What are you afraid of? Write about that.

Got any funny personal stories? Maybe you lost your bathing suit in the ocean or accidentally sneezed all over your teacher one time? C'mon, out with it!

What's the most embarrassing and funny thing you have done in public? _____

_____

_____

What's the most embarrassing and funny thing one of your **family members** has done in public?

_____

_____

_____

What's the most embarrassing and funny thing you've seen happen in public? _____

_____

_____

Are you a **Dancing Machine**? Doesn't matter. You still need to have a *signature dance move*, preferably one that has people laughing hysterically. Write its name and origin story, of course.

_____

_____

_____

_____

_____

_____

_____

_____

_____

_____

Now show us how to **WORK THAT THANG**. (Sorry.) Draw your dance move using stick figures with instructions on how to do it.

Wouldja not take a shower for an entire week?
YES or **NO**

Wouldja fake cry throughout an entire rollercoaster ride?
YES or **NO**

Wouldja shave your head on a whim?
YES or **NO**

Wouldja put a giant spider in your sister's underwear drawer?
YES or **NO**

Select your favorite and least favorite question from the previous page. Did you respond **YES** or **NO**? Write about your answers and explain why you would (or wouldn't) do the activity.

_____

_____

_____

_____

_____

_____

_____

_____

_____

_____

_____

Create four totally **new and crazy words**. Make sure to define their meanings too. Then start using them with your friends, and see what happens. Is "bleefing" a thing? It could be . . .

_____

_____

_____

_____

_____

_____

_____

_____

_____

_____

Now write a dialogue between two characters using your new words from the previous page.

_____

_____

_____

_____

_____

_____

_____

_____

_____

_____

_____

_____

Create five hilarious and totally original acronyms (you know, like **LOL**). Make sure you mention what they stand for too!

1.

2.

3.

4.

5.

Draw a FOOT. Is it gross? Is it hilariously large?
Are its nails crazy long?

Wouldja run through your school dressed
as an insane clown? **YES** or **NO**

Wouldja carry a jar of goo around school and refer to
it as "my best bud, Barry"? **YES** or **NO**

Wouldja argue with an invisible person in a public place?
YES or **NO**

Wouldja drink a VERY warm soda? **YES** or **NO**

Select your favorite and least favorite question from the previous page. Did you respond **YES** or **NO**? Write about your answers and explain why you would (or wouldn't) do the activity.

_____

_____

_____

_____

_____

_____

_____

_____

_____

_____

Write the rest of the story!

Barry knew something was wrong as soon as he stepped foot in the bathroom. The lights were low, but it didn't matter. But what he saw next would change his life FOREVER . . .

_____

_____

_____

_____

_____

_____

_____

_____

_____

_____

_____

_____

_____

_____

_____

_____

Fill in the blanks.

Fill in each blank with the type of word it requires.
Don't read ahead or think too much. Just do it!

As soon as I put my foot in the _____,
[noun]

I felt the _____ _____
[adjective]   [plural noun]

squishing around inside. I wanted to _____,
[verb]

but it was so gross I couldn't move. It was like a

million _____ eggs all hatched
[animal]

at once. That was the last summer I went

to Camp _____.
[adjective]

EVERYONE loves ice cream. But would they love it if the only flavor was SWEATY GYM SOCKS? Maybe not. Draw an advertisement for a brand-new ice cream flavor that'll have people talking.

Invent a crazy thing that **no one actually needs**. Something like a cat stroller (even though that's a real thing that **everyone** needs). Draw it here.

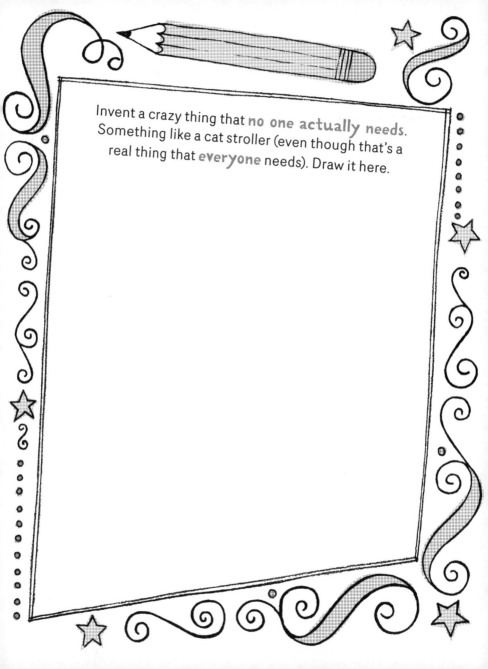

Have you ever had something so embarrassingly weird happen to you that it took a really long time to get over it? Can you laugh about it now? What kind of emotions does it bring up?

Have you ever exaggerated to make a story sound funnier?
Well, **NOW'S THE TIME!** Write about something funny that
happened to you, but pump it up to make it way more hysterical.

_____

_____

_____

_____

_____

_____

_____

_____

_____

_____

_____

_____

_____

_____

_____

_____

_____

_____

_____

List five weird secrets about yourself. GO!

1.

2.

3.

4.

5.

List five weird secrets you know
about other people.

1.

2.

3.

4.

5.

Fill in the blanks.

Fill in each blank with the type of word it requires.
Don't read ahead or think too much. **Just do it**!

"_____! Get in this house, you little
        [your name]

_____!" Mom shouted. "You left
        [animal]

a plate of _____ in here, and it's
              [plural noun]

getting _____. I am your mother,
            [adjective]

not your _____. Now clean your
              [job title]

_____, and start _____!"
        [noun]   [verb ending in ing]

What if you ate a magic apple that made you smell like apple pie for the rest of your life? Would you tell the world for fame or keep it on the DL? Write about it.

_____

_____

_____

_____

_____

_____

_____

_____

_____

_____

_____

_____

_____

_____

How do you build a snowman? Does it come alive when no one is looking? That's freaky. Draw four funny panels about the birth of a snowman.

Would you rather become super famous for doing something good **OR** become super rich by doing something mean?

Would you rather take a job you don't like **OR** take a job you love for free?

Would you rather swim in a dirty pool for ten minutes **OR** stick your hand up a cow's butt?

Write the **first thing** that pops into your brain after each word. Don't think about it.

Party
_____

Bummed
_____

Silly
_____

Boat
_____

Plus
_____

Moss
_____

Quirky
_____

Flip
_____

Take a good hard look at your answers on the previous page, and really THINK about them. Do you know why you wrote down the words that you did? Figure out your thought process, and try to justify some of your responses.

_____

_____

_____

_____

_____

_____

_____

_____

_____

_____

_____

_____

_____

Come up with five really funny PUNS. Oh, you don't know what a pun is? Then you better look it up.

1.

2.

3.

4.

5.

Write the rest of the story!

"Where is the scepter, peasant?!?!" the evil queen screamed. She gazed around the room, noticing nothing but dirty clothes. Suddenly, a red glow appeared under a pile of underwear. Her eyes wide, she stuck her hand in the pile and gasped . . .

_____

_____

_____

_____

_____

_____

_____

_____

_____

_____

_____

_____

_____

_____

_____

_____

List your top five funniest viral videos!

1.

2.

3.

4.

5.

Do you have a favorite **viral video star** whom you think is pretty freakin' hilarious? Write about them a little. What do they do that makes them so funny?

_____

_____

_____

_____

_____

_____

_____

_____

Wouldja call in sick to school and say it's because your "tummy feels icky"? **YES** or **NO**

Wouldja invite your friends over for breakfast and serve them uncooked wieners? **YES** or **NO**

Wouldja get into a perfume squirt-off in a mall department store? **YES** or **NO**

Wouldja wear a big photograph of your cat around your neck for a week? **YES** or **NO**

Select your favorite and least favorite question from the previous page. Did you respond **YES** or **NO**? Write about your answers and explain why you would (or wouldn't) do the activity.

_____

_____

_____

_____

_____

_____

_____

_____

_____

_____

Write the rest of the story!

As a thousand cyborg jellyfish began moving toward him, Biff knew his vacation wouldn't be as relaxing as he originally thought. Then he saw the one thing that would make him swim for the shore . . .

_____

_____

_____

_____

_____

_____

_____

_____

_____

_____

_____

_____

_____

_____

_____

_____

Find a **weird-looking doll** or action figure and DRAW IT in an exaggerated way as if it was ALIVE.

Name a few funny situations that you hope never happen to you but that you'd secretly love to watch your friends try to deal with.

_____

_____

_____

_____

_____

_____

_____

_____

_____

_____

_____

_____

_____

_____

_____

_____

_____

Let's pretend for a moment that you're a mad scientist who has just invented some screwball device that will change the world. Write about it all below!

_____

_____

_____

_____

_____

_____

_____

_____

_____

_____

_____

_____

_____

_____

_____

_____

_____

_____

What funny things **inspire** you? Use this space to doodle whatever that might be.

Write the rest of the story!

We all hid under the blanket, waiting patiently for Tim to return from school so we could scare the pants off of him. Little did we know that Tim would end up scaring us WAY more than we would scare him. And it all started with one little thing . . .

_____

_____

_____

_____

_____

_____

_____

_____

_____

_____

_____

_____

_____

_____

_____

_____

_____

_____

Wouldja not change your sheets for a month?
YES or **NO**

Wouldja put your nail clippings in a jar and
mark it "angel wings"? **YES** or **NO**

Wouldja have a lively conversation with yourself
while sitting alone at a restaurant? **YES** or **NO**

Wouldja not replace the toilet paper and write
"Sowwy!" on the empty roll? **YES** or **NO**

Select your favorite and least favorite question from the previous page. Did you respond **YES** or **NO**? Write about your answers and explain why you would (or wouldn't) do the activity.

_____

_____

_____

_____

_____

_____

_____

_____

_____

_____

Do you ever sing when you're alone and imagine you're a charismatic superstar who commands audiences with your amazing voice? You should. It's fun. But it's funnier if you do it in public. Give it a shot, then write about the experience.

_____
_____
_____
_____
_____
_____
_____
_____
_____
_____
_____
_____
_____
_____
_____
_____
_____
_____
_____

It's fun to trick people sometimes. Like telling your little sister she's actually a robot! She'll believe just about anything. List five simple tricks to play on your friends and family.

1.

2.

3.

4.

5.

What is a funny fear that you **have**?

_____

_____

What's a funny fear that you've **heard about**?

_____

_____

What's a funny fear that you **wish you had**?

_____

_____

What is the weirdest item that you **own**?

What is the weirdest item that you've ever **seen for sale**?

What is the weirdest item that your friend owns and you **secretly want**?

Write the **first thing** that pops into your brain after each word. Don't think about it.

Bae

Ship

Family

Chill

Flex

Butter

Love

Real

Take a good hard look at your answers on the previous page, and really **THINK** about them. Do you know why you wrote down the words that you did? Figure out your thought process, and try to justify some of your responses.

_____

_____

_____

_____

_____

_____

_____

_____

_____

_____

_____

What are five of the funniest fibs you might tell your friends and family about yourself? Don't go overboard. Keep 'em nice and weird.

1.

2.

3.

4.

5.

The hottest new trend these days is a **TOP HAT PARTY. JK.**
But you should create a hilarious new trend that makes
no sense but that people **LOVE** (for about a week).

_____

_____

_____

_____

_____

_____

_____

_____

_____

_____

_____

_____

_____

_____

_____

_____

_____

_____

Design a goofball superhero who'd rather bumble around all day than fight crime. Remember, even a clumsy lame-o can still have a warrior spirit!

Draw yourself at 100 years old. Use a current photo for reference, and then add A LOT of **wrinkles**.

Wouldja post an embarrassing photo
of yourself online? **YES** or **NO**

Wouldja go to a fancy dinner and pretend you're
not worthy enough to eat fancy foods? **YES** or **NO**

Wouldja ever challenge your mom to a
dance competition? **YES** or **NO**

Wouldja wear a crown and cape to a jewelry store and tell
the manager, "Show me your shiniest stuff!" **YES** or **NO**

Select your favorite and least favorite question from the previous page. Did you respond **YES** or **NO**? Write about your answers and explain why you would (or wouldn't) do the activity.

_____

_____

_____

_____

_____

_____

_____

_____

_____

_____

Fill in the blanks.

Fill in each blank with the type of word it requires.
Don't read ahead or think too much. **Just do it!**

It was 7 a.m. and there was a giant

_____ on my lawn. It was
        [noun]

_____ like a/an _____
      [adjective]   [noun]

and humming like a bird. It had tiny little

_____ all over it that were
   [plural noun]

pretty _____. We tried to
         [adjective]

_____ it but had no luck so we called
      [verb]

it a/an _____ and went back to bed.
       [noun]

What if you found out you could be the most successful person EVER but only if you did a job you hate for the rest of your life. Would you do it? Write about why you would . . . or wouldn't.

You know what's funny? **Smells**. Try creating one yourself
(NOT THAT WAY). Carefully select a combination of scents
to create a **fragrant masterpiece**. Describe your
experimental process, and then give your odor a name and
a witty tag line. Does that make SCENTS? (Sorry!)

_____

_____

_____

_____

_____

_____

_____

_____

_____

Fill this page with circles. **Draw BIG circles** and **LITTLE circles** and **MEDIUM-SIZE circles**. Lots and lots of circles. Use some color too while you're at it.

Can you remember back to when you were a little kid?
What's your funniest childhood memory?
Write about it in as much detail as you can recall.

Have you ever **farted loudly** in public?
Did people hear it and react?

Have you ever sneezed so hard you covered yourself
in **snot**? Did people watch?

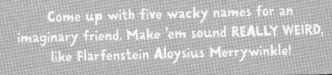

Come up with five wacky names for an imaginary friend. Make 'em sound **REALLY WEIRD**, like Flarfenstein Aloysius Merrywinkle!

1.

2.

3.

4.

5.

Select your favorite name from the previous page, and create a whole backstory! Where are they from? What's their catchphrase? Make it SUPER weird.

Draw the most mesmerizing and insane hairstyle you can think of using crayons, pencils, or markers.

What if you woke up one day in a stranger's body AND that stranger was super rich and famous? Would you tell people right away? Would you FREAK OUT? What would you do?

_____

_____

_____

_____

_____

_____

_____

_____

_____

_____

_____

_____

_____

_____

What if you walked in on your favorite celebrity in the **bathroom**? Would you wait till they came out and *apologize* to them OR never say anything? Write about your possible reactions.

_____

_____

_____

_____

_____

_____

_____

_____

_____

_____

How do you make a cupcake? Wait a minute. Don't cupcakes come from the sky? Hmmm. Why don't you show us THE TRUTH in four steps?

Would you rather let a rat crawl all over your body **OR** take a nap with a snake?

Would you rather wear a big coat all summer long **OR** wear shorts all winter long?

Would you rather live in a big city by yourself **OR** on a small island packed with people?

What are five weird things that would be really cool if you could get them from a vending machine? Like pumpkin bread! That could be delicious.

1.

2.

3.

4.

5.

Write the first thing that pops into your brain after each word. Don't think about it.

Swerve

_____

Mega

_____

Busted

_____

Ghost

_____

Support

_____

Ham

_____

Boost

_____

Dude

_____

Take a good hard look at your answers on the previous page, and really THINK about them. Do you know why you wrote down the words that you did? Figure out your thought process, and try to justify some of your responses.

Write a funny pen-pal letter to your past self. What advice would you give yourself? Would "younger" you be jealous of what "current" you is up to? If not, MAKE YOURSELF SUPER JEALOUS.

Imagine you've been asked to speak at graduation because you're super wise. Write a funny speech that's filled with wisdom about life after school, and make sure it keeps people awake!

_____

_____

_____

_____

_____

_____

_____

_____

_____

_____

_____

_____

_____

_____

_____

_____

_____

_____

Time to work on your **fitness**! Create a weirdo new *exercise craze*. Give it a name, and write about it. Oh, make sure you don't hurt yourself in the process. That's important.

_____

_____

_____

_____

_____

_____

_____

_____

_____

_____

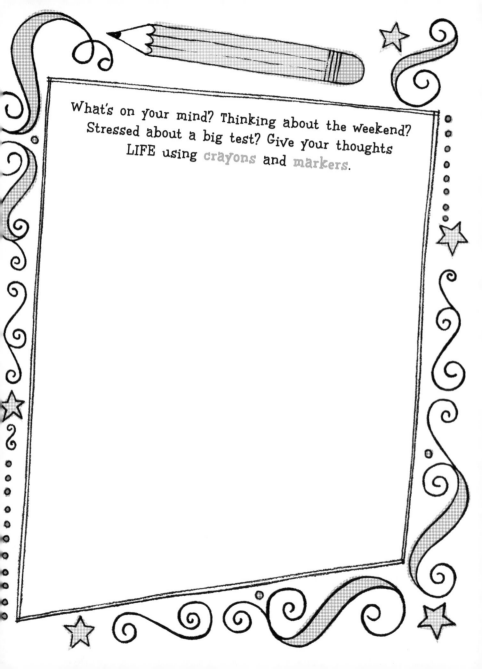

What's on your mind? Thinking about the weekend? Stressed about a big test? Give your thoughts LIFE using crayons and markers.

Fill in the blanks.

Fill in each blank with the type of word it requires.
Don't read ahead or think too much. Just do it!

Grandma sat her dusty old _____
[noun]

on the counter. It smelled like _____
[adjective]

_____. I stared at it all day until
[plural noun]

a/an _____ broke into the house
[animal]

and ate it. We tried to _____
[verb]

the smell out of the _____ but
[plural noun]

it didn't work. Grandma was pretty mad.

Do you ever remember stuff as being WAY funnier than reality? Happens all the time. Think hard and write down stuff that might not have been the knee-slapper you originally thought it was.

Have you ever experienced a "Secret Funny"?
Like maybe your friend farted at lunch and
no one heard it but you? Write about a few of them.

_____

_____

_____

_____

_____

_____

_____

_____

_____

_____

_____

_____

_____

_____

_____

_____

_____

_____

Draw a crazy joke-telling robot whose
mission it is to make you laugh.

Wouldja post a photo of yourself
sitting on the toilet to social media?
YES or **NO**

Wouldja eat a dog treat in front of your
dog just to make it jealous?
YES or **NO**

Wouldja go on a road trip to your favorite place in
the whole world . . . with your parents?
YES or **NO**

Wouldja dress up like the Easter Bunny on Halloween?
YES or **NO**

Select your favorite and least favorite question from the previous page. Did you respond **YES** or **NO**? Write about your answers and explain why you would (or wouldn't) do the activity.

_____

_____

_____

_____

_____

_____

_____

_____

_____

_____

_____

Draw a humorous sign. It can be about ANYTHING. Just make it funny.

Write a few funny haikus! Don't worry, it's simple. The first line is five syllables, the second line is seven syllables, and the third line is five syllables. Choose a few strange topics, and go for it.

Create a funny fake charity for people to champion, like "Save the Cupcakes!" Write a mission statement and a platform so people can take action.

What is the funniest video game that you can think of?

_____

What's the funniest **app** that you use?

_____

What's the funniest board game that you've played?

_____

Write the **first thing** that pops into your brain after each word. Don't think about it.

Odd
_____

Peanut
_____

Bounce
_____

Medium
_____

Antics
_____

Pizza
_____

Goofy
_____

Sauce
_____

Take a good hard look at your answers on the previous page, and really **THINK** about them. Do you know why you wrote down the words that you did? Figure out your thought process, and try to justify some of your responses.

_____

_____

_____

_____

_____

_____

_____

_____

_____

_____

_____

_____

_____

What's the weirdest **current trend** that you think is totally hilarious?

What's the weirdest **old school trend** that you think is totally hilarious?

What's the weirdest trend that you have **no idea** why people like?

Come up with three FUNNY (and maybe a little WEIRD)
things to do when you're at dinner with your family.
Nothing that would get you in major trouble though.
DANGER = BAD.

_____

_____

_____

_____

_____

_____

_____

_____

_____

_____

_____

_____

_____

_____

_____

_____

_____

_____

Fill in the blanks.

Fill in each blank with the type of word it requires. Don't read ahead or think too much. **Just do it**!

It's always a/an _____ day when I

[adjective]

don't get my _____ in the morning.

[noun]

A good _____ is so important.

[noun]

Especially if you want to _____.

[verb]

Be careful though. Too many _____

[plural noun]

can make you feel _____.

[adjective]

Gotta have my _____!

[noun]

What's your **funniest facial feature?**
DRAW IT! And make it even more hilarious.

Choose a person whom you know (and like) but don't know TOO much about. Write a quick biography about them using funny facts you made up about their life.

_____

_____

_____

_____

_____

_____

_____

_____

_____

_____

_____

_____

_____

_____

_____

_____

Design a book cover for the biography you
just created. Is it kind of creepy since
you don't actually know the person all that well?
Maybe a little. But that's okay.

Who's the funniest person in your family?
What makes them so hilarious? Write about them
and their hysterical nature.

_____

_____

_____

_____

_____

_____

_____

_____

_____

_____

_____

_____

_____

_____

_____

_____

_____

_____

Do you have a particularly funny teacher? How do they keep class light and fun? Write about why you think (or don't think) humor helps you learn more.

_____

_____

_____

_____

_____

_____

_____

_____

_____

_____

_____

_____

_____

_____

_____

_____

_____

Walk into a **packed classroom** and say, "THE PARTY MASTER HAS ARRIVED. LET'S GET FREAKY!" Write about what happened next.

_____

_____

_____

_____

_____

_____

_____

_____

_____

When you walk by a restaurant window, point and say in a very loud voice, "A HUMAN ZOO?! What will they think of next?!?!" Record the patrons' reactions, and write about the experience.

_____

_____

_____

_____

_____

_____

_____

_____

_____

_____

_____

_____

_____

_____

_____

_____

_____

How do you brush your teeth?
SHOW US WITH PICTURES. You've got four panels.
Use them wisely. And make it funny!

Would you rather have a gigantic zit on the end of your nose **OR** fry your hair with bleach?

Would you rather ask a stranger out on a date **OR** tell a good friend you have a crush on them?

Would you rather get stung by a jellyfish **OR** get stung by a bee?

Write the **first thing** that pops into your brain after each word. Don't think about it.

Toast
_____

Arrow
_____

Iced
_____

Museum
_____

Hawk
_____

Compassion
_____

Entertain
_____

Rot
_____

Take a good hard look at your answers on the previous page, and really THINK about them. Do you know why you wrote down the words that you did? Figure out your thought process, and try to justify some of your responses.

_____

_____

_____

_____

_____

_____

_____

_____

_____

_____

_____

_____

Do you have a hidden talent that no one else knows about? Well, it's time to unleash the creative beast that lives inside you! Write about your secret talent and why you don't share it with anyone.

_____

_____

_____

_____

_____

_____

_____

_____

_____

_____

_____

_____

_____

_____

_____

Draw a crazy new type of fun-loving animal that everyone will think is cute and funny. Extra points if it's a little bit dangerous.

Fill in the blanks.

Fill in each blank with the type of word it requires. Don't read ahead or think too much. **Just do it!**

"Who's there!?" shouted Madeline. She tried

to _____ the door but it didn't
          [verb]

work. A big white _____ dropped
                       [noun]

from the ceiling onto her shoulder. "Ahhh!

_____ are _____.
   [plural noun]   [adjective]

Get it off!" We quickly grabbed the

_____ and ran to the sheriff for help.
     [noun]

Choose a song with really **lame lyrics**. Take a good hard look at it, and then switch up the lyrics so that the song becomes SUPER hilarious.

_____

_____

_____

_____

_____

_____

_____

_____

_____

_____

Oh well, I guess you just think you're an expert on EVERYTHING, don't you? That's cool. So why don't you choose a subject you know NOTHING about and write about it like you're an expert?

_____

_____

_____

_____

_____

_____

_____

_____

_____

_____

_____

_____

_____

_____

_____

_____

_____

_____

Name five funny people whom you'd love to have dinner with.

1.

2.

3.

4.

5.

Now write a totally new joke from scratch!
Don't freak out. It's kind of hard. But why not give it a try?
Experiment a little, get loose, and have fun.

Draw your own **funny Internet meme!**
Make sure its ULTRA original and hilarious.

Draw the **craziest outfit** you can think of
and make it totally INSANE.

What's a funny tradition that you grew up with?

Where did it come from?

_____

_____

_____

_____

What's a funny older tradition you've heard about?

Do you know how it started?

_____

_____

_____

_____

What's the funniest question you've ever been **asked**?
What did you answer?

What's the funniest question you've ever
asked someone? What did they answer?

Fill in the blanks.

Fill in each blank with the type of word it requires. Don't read ahead or think too much. **Just do it**!

When I won the Golden _____
[noun]

Award, I knew things would change. Life would

be more _____! I'd get free
[adjective]

_____ whenever I wanted. I'd
[plural noun]

never have to _____ again. But
[verb]

too many _____ made me feel
[plural noun]

_____ so I gave it back. End of story.
[adjective]

What if you became best friends with an old sorceress?
Would you bring her over to your house? Would you want
to see her cast evil spells, or is that weird?
Write about your friendship and how it works.

_____
_____
_____
_____
_____
_____
_____
_____
_____
_____
_____
_____
_____
_____
_____
_____
_____

How do you get your hair to look SO GOOD?
Draw your process in the panels below. Reveal your secrets
through ART! (Or something.)

Write the **first thing** that pops into your brain after each word. Don't think about it.

Plump

_____

Message

_____

Table

_____

Square

_____

Character

_____

Adventure

_____

Rocket

_____

Kitten

_____

Take a good hard look at your answers on the previous page, and really **THINK** about them. Do you know why you wrote down the words that you did? Figure out your thought process, and try to justify some of your responses.

_____

_____

_____

_____

_____

_____

_____

_____

_____

_____

_____

_____

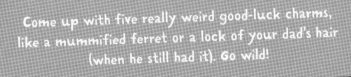

Come up with five really weird good-luck charms, like a mummified ferret or a lock of your dad's hair (when he still had it). Go wild!

1.

2.

3.

4.

5.

Write the rest of the story!

Bonnie watched Lonnie for hours. She couldn't stop. He was THAT good. Some even say he was the best dancer at St. Aloysius. Lonnie jumped up and landed on the ground in a split formation. Bonnie gasped when she realized . . .

_____

_____

_____

_____

_____

_____

_____

_____

_____

_____

_____

_____

_____

_____

_____

_____

_____

Wouldja shout, "I HATE WEARING PANTS!"
on a crowded bus? **YES** or **NO**

Wouldja tell an elderly person you'll be their
helping hand if they give you a mint? **YES** or **NO**

Wouldja go to the grocery store, load your cart with
toilet paper, and then get in a very long checkout
line and say, "MOVE THIS THING ALONG!
I'M DYIN' OVER HERE!" **YES** or **NO**

Wouldja go to a department store's electronics section
and watch TV all day? **YES** or **NO**

Select your favorite and least favorite question from the previous page. Did you respond **YES** or **NO**? Write about your answers and explain why you would (or wouldn't) do the activity.

_____

_____

_____

_____

_____

_____

_____

_____

_____

_____

Write the rest of the story!

"I'm going to be a rapper!" mom shouted, moving her baseball cap to the side. She was wearing a sparkling silver tracksuit and holding a microphone. Things were about to take an unexpected turn . . .

_____

_____

_____

_____

_____

_____

_____

_____

_____

_____

_____

_____

_____

_____

_____

_____

_____

Your mom is a **rapper**! You know you want to draw that. Let's see what you've got.

Imagine you could have a meal with the funniest person you know. Explain why you chose them, what you'd talk about, and where you'd go to eat.

_____

_____

_____

_____

_____

_____

_____

_____

_____

_____

_____

_____

_____

_____

_____

_____

_____

Wouldja tell a stranger you love them and then run away out of sight? **YES** or **NO**

Wouldja cut in line while telling people, "I'm royalty, OK?" **YES** or **NO**

Wouldja purposely sing off key at a big event? **YES** or **NO**

Wouldja yell, "YEEEEEEEEE-HAW!" in the middle of the forest at night? **YES** or **NO**

Select your favorite and least favorite question from the previous page. Did you respond **YES** or **NO**? Write about your answers and explain why you would (or wouldn't) do the activity.

Write the **first thing** that pops into your brain after each word. Don't think about it.

Win
_____

Season
_____

Bond
_____

Dark
_____

Empathy
_____

Key
_____

Puppy
_____

Iron
_____

Take a good hard look at your answers on the previous page, and really **THINK** about them. Do you know why you wrote down the words that you did? Figure out your thought process, and try to justify some of your responses.

_____

_____

_____

_____

_____

_____

_____

_____

_____

_____

_____

_____

_____

Create a wacky new cartoon character that's all about slapstick humor. Give it a witty name too!

Have you ever heard one of your friends or family
make a really bad joke that people thought was too crude?
What happened next? Write about the experience below.

Wouldja wink at a crossing guard
and skip across the street? **YES** or **NO**

Wouldja go to a pizza parlor and ask,
"Which are the best pizzas to marry?" **YES** or **NO**

Wouldja tell a friend's baby that it's ugly? **YES** or **NO**

Wouldja pretend you don't know
English at the drive-thru? **YES** or **NO**

Select your favorite and least favorite question from the previous page. Did you respond **YES** or **NO**? Write about your answers and explain why you would (or wouldn't) do the activity.

_____

_____

_____

_____

_____

_____

_____

_____

_____

_____

_____

1.

2.

3.

4.

5.

Yoga can be weird. Someone had to say it. Why don't you draw a new yoga pose and try to make your friends do it? Name it something funny like "The Soft Pretzel," and then write about it below.

Find a nice, clear photograph of yourself, and then draw it in an abstract way. Make it **geometrical**, and **emphasize the lines**. Look up different types of abstract paintings for help if you need to.

Write the rest of the story!

As I opened my eyes I could see I was no longer on Earth. The air was thick, and the site was covered in tiny creatures I couldn't identify. They began biting me, but I mostly brushed them off. It was pretty scary but not as scary as what happened next...

_____

_____

_____

_____

_____

_____

_____

_____

_____

_____

_____

_____

_____

_____

_____

_____

How do you fall asleep at night? Do you drift off into slumberland OR toss and turn till you pass out? You've got four panels to show the world. Make 'em good.

What are five really funny rules that MUST be followed when someone comes into your room? Come up with some good ones OR ELSE.

1.

2.

3.

4.

5.

Would you rather milk an angry cow
OR milk an angry goat?

Would you rather have your body be covered entirely in
hair **OR** have no ability to grow body hair whatsoever?

Would you rather throw a surprise party **OR** have a
surprise party thrown for you?

Fill in the blanks.

Fill in each blank with the type of word it requires.
Don't read ahead or think too much. **Just do it!**

I stepped into the bathroom right as the

_____ began shooting straight
[type of liquid]

up into the air. It covered the whole place!

Talk about _____. I had to use a/
[adjective]

an _____ to _____
[noun]   [verb]

everything, and it still smelled like

_____ _____ for weeks.
[adjective]   [food item]

Write the **first thing** that pops into your brain after each word. Don't think about it.

Bubble

_____

Creep

_____

Guide

_____

Active

_____

Teamwork

_____

Scout

_____

Coffee

_____

Vacation

_____

Take a good hard look at your answers on the previous page, and really **THINK** about them. Do you know why you wrote down the words that you did? Figure out your thought process, and try to justify some of your responses.

_____

_____

_____

_____

_____

_____

_____

_____

_____

_____

_____

Write the rest of the story!

Dan's stomach was grumbling so loud that everyone in the neighborhood could hear. He closed his eyes and hoped the feeling would go away. But it didn't. Suddenly . . .

_____

_____

_____

_____

_____

_____

_____

_____

_____

_____

_____

_____

_____

_____

Write an odd letter to an alien pen pal. Reminisce about hilarious times you two shared, and make some plans to hang out again next time he or she is on Earth.

You just won a VERY PRESTIGIOUS award. That's awesome! Write your acceptance speech, and make up a bunch of funny and weird facts about what you did to win.

Would you rather be covered in slime **OR** moldy cheese?

Would you rather kiss a moose **OR** kiss a llama?

Would you rather drink a glass of mud **OR** lick the dust off everything in your house?

Create a hilarious (but not NEFARIOUS) prank to
play on one of your closest friends. Then write about the
experience after you do it. Nothing nasty though. Be cool!

What are your top five funniest movies of all time? This is a tough one. So many good ones! Think hard but don't stress. Maybe you should watch some classics to prepare yourself!

1.

2.

3.

4.

5.

Draw the ugliest **hat** you can imagine.

Make an INSANE face. Then take a photograph of yourself making that face. Now draw a picture of the photograph of you making that face.

Write the rest of the story!

The teacher brought out a metal box adorned with a gigantic clown face. What was inside? No one knew. She took the lid off to reveal something no one expected to see . . .

_____

_____

_____

_____

_____

_____

_____

_____

_____

_____

_____

_____

_____

_____

_____

_____

_____

What was inside the box? Draw it, silly.
DRAW IT ALL.

What would happen if you woke up in your best friend's body? How would you spend your day? Would you snoop around and cause trouble or act like nothing was wrong? Write about how you'd handle it.

_____
_____
_____
_____
_____
_____
_____
_____
_____
_____
_____
_____
_____
_____
_____
_____

How do you make a pizza? You just sprinkle
some magic dust on a pepperoni! Right? Probably.
You've got four panels to figure it out.

Would you rather go without TV for a year **OR** go without your favorite comfort food for a year?

Would you rather live in a jumpy castle for a month **OR** sleep in a dog's bed for a week?

Would you rather write a sweet poem to your worst enemy **OR** write a mean poem to your best friend?

Draw something **HILARIOUS**.
It can be ANYTHING that pops into your brain.

Write the **first thing** that pops into your brain after each word. Don't think about it.

Superior

_____

Gain

_____

Cheer

_____

Target

_____

Girl

_____

Regular

_____

Cast

_____

Erase

_____

Take a good hard look at your answers on the previous page, and really **THINK** about them. Do you know why you wrote down the words that you did? Figure out your thought process, and try to justify some of your responses.

_____

_____

_____

_____

_____

_____

_____

_____

_____

_____

_____

_____

Fill in the blanks.

Fill in each blank with the type of word it requires. Don't read ahead or think too much. **Just do it**!

"Bad news," the doctor said. "I can't see

your _____ because it's too
        [noun]

_____. We're going to have to
      [adjective]

use the _____ and operate on
              [noun]

it. It might be a little _____ so
                          [adjective]

grab a/an _____ and get ready to
              [noun]

_____. This won't hurt a bit."
      [verb]

If you could go on a crazy space adventure and could choose four friends to come with you, who would they be and why? Oh, and pets count as friends!

How does a caterpillar become a butterfly?
Interpret this unique metamorphosis in a hilarious way
via the four panels below.

Spend an entire day in silence. Don't speak to ANYONE. Go to the grocery store, the mall, or wherever. Interact with a lot of people, but stay totally zipped. Write about the experience.

_____

_____

_____

_____

_____

_____

_____

_____

_____

_____

_____

_____

_____

_____

_____

_____

_____

_____

Come up with five weird and funny titles
for a children's picture book.

1.

2.

3.

4.

5.

Choose one of the book titles you just came up with, and draw a cover for it!

Write the rest of the story!

Winnie wasn't just a teen sorceress; she was also a baker. And the cupcakes she was serving had an extra sprinkle of magic in them. Everyone at the party began to change into . . .

_____

_____

_____

_____

_____

_____

_____

_____

_____

_____

_____

_____

_____

_____

_____

_____

_____

_____

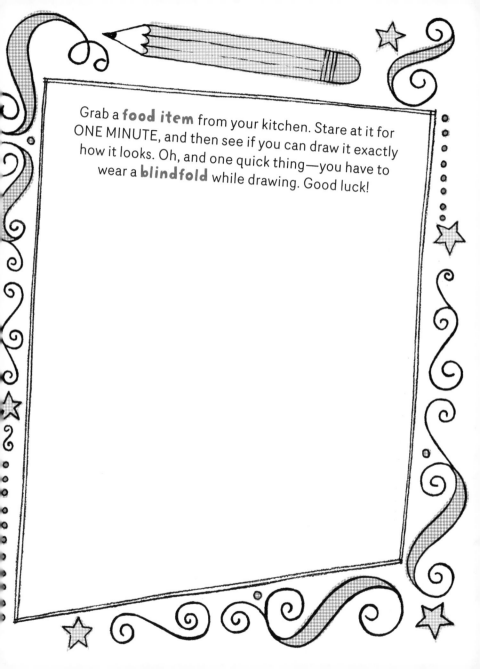

Grab a **food item** from your kitchen. Stare at it for ONE MINUTE, and then see if you can draw it exactly how it looks. Oh, and one quick thing—you have to wear a **blindfold** while drawing. Good luck!

What is the funniest place you've ever **been**?

_____

_____

What is the funniest place you've **heard about**?

_____

_____

What is the funniest place you **hope to go** someday?

_____

_____

When was the last time you died with **laughter**?

What was it about? _____

_____

When was the last time you **made someone** die
from laughter? What did you do or say?

_____

_____

When was the last time you **made an adult**
laugh even though they might not have wanted
to? What happened? _____

_____

_____

Halloween is the **PERFECT** time for a good prank.
Come up with a couple spooky and hilarious tricks
to play on any unsuspecting trick-or-treaters
who might stop by your house.

Since we're on the Halloween theme, just go ahead and design a pumpkin while you're at it. YOU KNOW YOU WANT TO. Make it funny and frightening.

How do you blow a bubble? Show the world
in four easy steps! This could get messy.

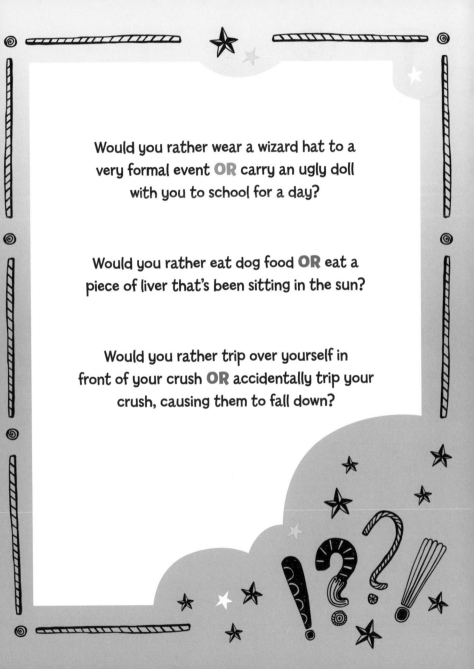

Would you rather wear a wizard hat to a very formal event **OR** carry an ugly doll with you to school for a day?

Would you rather eat dog food **OR** eat a piece of liver that's been sitting in the sun?

Would you rather trip over yourself in front of your crush **OR** accidentally trip your crush, causing them to fall down?

Write the **first thing** that pops into your brain after each word. Don't think about it.

Swag

_____

Hamster

_____

Bones

_____

Cereal

_____

Reality

_____

Wash

_____

Follow

_____

Joke

_____

Take a good hard look at your answers on the previous page, and really **THINK** about them. Do you know why you wrote down the words that you did? Figure out your thought process, and try to justify some of your responses.

_____

_____

_____

_____

_____

_____

_____

_____

_____

_____

_____

What are five landmarks you can think of off the top of your head?

1.

2.

3.

4.

5.

What's the weirdest object you own? Is there a crazy story behind it? If there isn't one, make it up!

_____

_____

_____

_____

_____

_____

_____

_____

_____

_____

_____

_____

_____

_____

_____

_____

_____

_____

Have you ever tried writing a **comedy sketch?** Write one now! Start with two characters, figure out what each of them wants in the scene, and then throw some obstacles in their way. It's a tough challenge, but you can handle it.

_____

_____

_____

_____

_____

_____

_____

_____

_____

_____

_____

_____

(You're probably going to need this space for your sketch.
It's all good.)

_____

_____

_____

_____

_____

_____

_____

_____

_____

_____

_____

_____

You've been chosen to give a speech at your best friend's wedding. All eyes are on you! Better tell a few funny stories to keep people from pouncing on that giant wedding cake.

_____

_____

_____

_____

_____

_____

_____

_____

_____

_____

_____

_____

_____

_____

_____

_____

_____

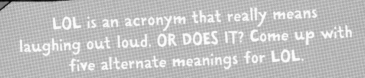

LOL is an acronym that really means laughing out loud. OR DOES IT? Come up with five alternate meanings for LOL.

1.

2.

3.

4.

5.

You're the **PRESIDENT OF THE WORLD**. Come up with a hilarious thing to be passionate about. Puppies' rights? Putting soft serve ice cream in every high school? **GO FOR IT, PREZ!**

Have you ever stayed awake **ALL NIGHT**? What was the latest you've ever stayed up? How did it feel? Write about it in detail.

_____
_____
_____
_____
_____
_____
_____
_____
_____
_____
_____
_____
_____
_____
_____
_____
_____
_____

Wouldja tell your brother
he's actually your clone? **YES** or **NO**

Wouldja run into a clothing store at the mall and
scream, "IT'S PROM SEASON AND MAMA NEEDS SOME
HELP!" **YES** or **NO**

Wouldja ask someone who works at the grocery store
if their milk came from "gifted" cows? **YES** or **NO**

Wouldja tell your teacher you were late to class
because of "some crazy twisters!"? **YES** or **NO**

Select your favorite and least favorite question from the previous page. Did you respond **YES** or **NO**? Write about your answers and explain why you would (or wouldn't) do the activity.

_____

_____

_____

_____

_____

_____

_____

_____

_____

_____

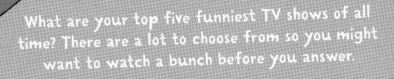

What are your top five funniest TV shows of all time? There are a lot to choose from so you might want to watch a bunch before you answer.

1.

2.

3.

4.

5.

Name five of the weirdest jobs you can think of off the top of your head. **GO!**

1.

2.

3.

4.

5.

What's a funny rumor that you've heard about **yourself**?_____

_____

_____

What's a funny rumor that you've heard about **a friend**? _____

_____

_____

What's a funny rumor that turned out to be **totally true**?_____

_____

_____

Sometimes rumors can actually be kind of funny. Try spreading a weird rumor about yourself but tell only a few people. See how long it takes to spread, and then write about the experience here.

Draw the most miserable-looking cat
in the entire world.

Think of the absolute worst outfit ON THE PLANET. Now draw it. Does it involve feathers? Probably.

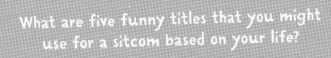

What are five funny titles that you might use for a sitcom based on your life?

1.

2.

3.

4.

5.

Imagine you created a TV show based on your life.
Who's in it? What is it about? Is it a story about a guy
and a girl who live underwater and have an octopus son?
Probably not . . . but it could be!

Write the **first thing** that pops into your brain after each word. Don't think about it.

Future

Comical

Buddy

Wrap

Morning

Foundation

Rich

Flake

Take a good hard look at your answers on the previous page, and really **THINK** about them. Do you know why you wrote down the words that you did? Figure out your thought process, and try to justify some of your responses.

Fill in the blanks.

Fill in each blank with the type of word it requires. Don't read ahead or think too much. **Just do it**!

When I see a/an _____ out in
[noun]

the open, it makes me so mad. It's like no

one even tried to _____. Plus,
[verb]

it makes everything _____,
[adjective]

like a/an _____ exploded.
[noun]

I wish we could just _____
[verb]

_____ like everyone else.
[plural noun]

What if you found out you're an immortal prince or princess from another realm? What would you do? Write about it.

_____

_____

_____

_____

_____

_____

_____

_____

_____

_____

_____

_____

_____

_____

How do you become a clown? Besides hard work,
of course! Show the universe how to paint your face
in four easy panels. Oooh, this should be good.

What are your top five funniest cartoons of all time? They can be TV shows OR movies as long as they make you ROFL.

1.

2.

3.

4.

5.

Would you rather smell like poop all day **OR** vomit in a public place for all to see?

Would you rather tell your teacher that you wet your pants **OR** suck your thumb like a baby for an entire class period?

Would you rather wear a flesh-colored bodysuit to school **OR** wear clown makeup for an entire weekend?

Fill in the blanks.

Fill in each blank with the type of word it requires.
Don't read ahead or think too much. **Just do it**!

The waiter set down a heaping plate of

_____ in front of us. It was
　　　　[food item]

covered in _____ and had
　　　　　　　　[plural noun]

a/an _____ aroma. As we
　　　　　[adjective]

began to _____ it, a gigantic
　　　　　　　　[verb]

_____ poked its head out
　　　[animal]

of the pile and grinned. I grabbed my

_____ and bolted!
　　　[clothing item]

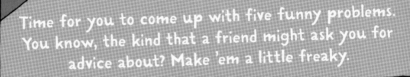

Time for you to come up with five funny problems. You know, the kind that a friend might ask you for advice about? Make 'em a little freaky.

1.

2.

3.

4.

5.

Are you good at giving advice? Sure hope not because today you're going to give the worst advice EVER. Select a funny problem from the opposite page, and then give the worst possible advice.

_____

_____

_____

_____

_____

_____

_____

_____

_____

_____

_____

_____

_____

_____

_____

_____

Do you and your friends have lots of in-jokes and hilarious quotes? Write your favorite ones in the space below.

Fill in the blanks.

Fill in each blank with the type of word it requires. Don't read ahead or think too much. **Just do it**!

The ancient book was filled with so many

_____ secrets. Did you know
[adjective]

_____ was once a/an
[famous person]

_____ ? It's true. Also, a/an
[job title]

_____ has _____
[animal]   [number]

secret pouches so it can carry _____
[plural noun]

and food. The book also teaches you how to

_____ , but don't tell anyone.
[verb]

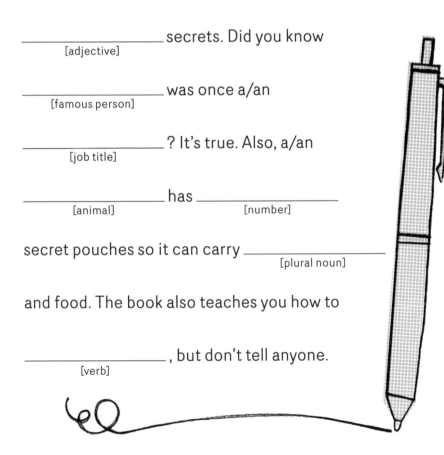

Write the **first thing** that pops into your brain after each word. Don't think about it.

Shoe

Grind

Homework

Clever

Upload

Cheese

Busted

Friend

Take a good hard look at your answers on the previous page, and really **THINK** about them. Do you know why you wrote down the words that you did? Figure out your thought process, and try to justify some of your responses.

_____

_____

_____

_____

_____

_____

_____

_____

_____

_____

_____

_____

_____

Write the rest of the story!

"You're late," Grandma whispered in my ear. The room lit up as classical music began to play and ballerinas quickly filed onto the stage one by one. Suddenly a loud roar came from behind the curtain as the ballerinas ran for their lives . . .

_____

_____

_____

_____

_____

_____

_____

_____

_____

_____

_____

_____

_____

_____

_____

_____

A meteor is headed straight for Earth. We have only an hour left to live, and now the president wants YOU to give a speech?! Time to write some famous last words. Make them humorous! People could probably use a good laugh . . .

You are the GALACTIC OVERLORD to the most
hilarious planet in the universe. Congrats! Create
your very own world to conquer. MAKE IT FUNNY.

The next time you karaoke, choose a rockin' song, and then sing it in a very soft voice (or a really bad voice). Watch how people react, and remember their responses. Write about the experience.

What are five songs that you think
are totally weird and funny?

1.

2.

3.

4.

5.

Go to a pet store, and pretend you think it's a restaurant.
Point at an animal, and ask if it comes with fries. Ask about the
specials! Write about the experience.

_____

_____

_____

_____

_____

_____

_____

_____

_____

_____

_____

_____

_____

Wouldja walk around a party with a plate of grapes and yell, "EYEBALLS! GETCHA SOME EYEBALLS HERE!" **YES** or **NO**

Wouldja go up to an info desk at the mall and tell them you need them to make an announcement because you lost "Mr. Binky"? **YES** or **NO**

Wouldja tell your guidance counselor you want to quit school to be a full-time rapper? **YES** or **NO**

Wouldja wear two different socks? **YES** or **NO**

Select your favorite and least favorite question from the previous page. Did you respond **YES** or **NO**? Write about your answers and explain why you would (or wouldn't) do the activity.

_____

_____

_____

_____

_____

_____

_____

_____

_____

_____

What's a weird thing that you collect?

_____

_____

What's a weird thing that your friends collect?

_____

_____

What's a weird thing that grandmas and grandpas

collect?_____

_____

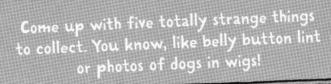

Come up with five totally strange things to collect. You know, like belly button lint or photos of dogs in wigs!

1.

2.

3.

4.

5.

Aliens have landed! YOU'VE been selected to speak with them. How lucky you are! Write a greeting to your new pals telling them how great Earth is and blahblahblah don't enslave us.

FREEZE! Now . . . stay that way. Pretend to be a mannequin in a store. Stay totally still. Pay attention to how people react and what they say. Write about the experience.

Time for a RANT. You can rant about anything you want as long as it's HI-LARIOUS.

You've been invited to an exotic costume party!
Design a weird and unique look that will leave people
with way more questions than answers.

Wouldja ask someone at the post
office how much it costs to send something
"INTO THE FUTURE"? **YES** or **NO**

Wouldja put on a bunch of really good fake tattoos
and tell your parents they're real? **YES** or **NO**

Wouldja give your teacher a bag of apples and say,
"These have always brought me luck!" **YES** or **NO**

Wouldja go to the ATM and yell, "I'M A WINNER!!!"
when your money came out? **YES** or **NO**

Select your favorite and least favorite question from the previous page. Did you respond **YES** or **NO**? Write about your answers and explain why you would (or wouldn't) do the activity.

_____

_____

_____

_____

_____

_____

_____

_____

_____

_____

_____

Write the **first thing** that pops into your brain after each word. Don't think about it.

Believe
_____

Future
_____

Pepper
_____

Sandwich
_____

Trip
_____

Witty
_____

Guide
_____

Jolly
_____

Take a good hard look at your answers on the previous page, and really **THINK** about them. Do you know why you wrote down the words that you did? Figure out your thought process, and try to justify some of your responses.

_____

_____

_____

_____

_____

_____

_____

_____

_____

_____

_____

Choose a day to try a bunch of totally new things. Taste a new food, or talk to someone you've never talked to before. Write about how it made you feel to step outside of your comfort zone.

_____
_____
_____
_____
_____
_____
_____
_____
_____
_____
_____
_____
_____
_____
_____
_____
_____
_____
_____

Walk around all day long carrying a briefcase (or folder) marked TOP SECRET. When people ask what's inside say, "I can't tell you that," and be super serious about it. Write about how people react.

Create your own language! It can be combinations of existing words, or it can be totally **made up gibberish**. Translate each of the words and phrases below.

Hello
_____

Good-bye
_____

Please
_____

Thank you
_____

Garbage
_____

Winner
_____

Now translate each of these very necessary phrases.

"Where is my hamster?"

_____

"Why is that robot so sad?"

_____

"Do not touch my shoulder!"

_____

"Your socks are ugly."

_____

"More liver and onions, old wizard."

_____

"Get out of here, Mom!"

_____

How do you catch a cold? Show the process by drawing in the four panels below, and feel free to make it crazy and weird.

List three weird types of dreams you're curious about. They say that if you have dreams about flying you might turn into an airplane. It's true! JK.

Wouldja tell a stranger you love them
and then skip into the distance? **YES** or **NO**

Wouldja go door to door singing
Christmas carols in June? **YES** or **NO**

Wouldja paint a picture of a horse and give it to your
best pal as a symbol of friendship? **YES** or **NO**

Wouldja eat all of the donuts in the house and then
leave a threatening note from "The Donut Patrol"?
YES or **NO**

Select your favorite and least favorite question from the previous page. Did you respond **YES** or **NO**? Write about your answers and explain why you would (or wouldn't) do the activity.

_____

_____

_____

_____

_____

_____

_____

_____

_____

_____

_____

Do you have any wacky good-luck charms?
Ooh, what are they? Write about them.

Spend some time watching different types of people interact in a public place. Observe people's behavior. Do young people act differently than older people? What makes people laugh?

Wouldja jump into a pool with
all your clothes on? **YES** or **NO**

Wouldja go to the deli counter at the grocery store
and say, "Tell me about each of these wondrous
pieces of meat, kind person!" **YES** or **NO**

Wouldja tell a stranger a secret
and then run away? **YES** or **NO**

Wouldja get up early to assemble a bunch of dolls at
the breakfast table so when everyone wakes up you
can say, "We've all been waiting for you!"? **YES** or **NO**

Select your favorite and least favorite question from the previous page. Did you respond **YES** or **NO**? Write about your answers and explain why you would (or wouldn't) do the activity.

It's time to lace up those dancin' shoes! Learn a dance (like the tango) with a friend (like your best one), and perform it in a public space (like the mall). Write about the experience.

What's the funniest job you can think of and why?
Would you do that job?

"Promposals" are kind of crazy, right? That's where someone goes to great lengths asking someone else to prom. Name three nutty promposal ideas to try.

_____

_____

_____

_____

_____

_____

_____

_____

_____

_____

_____

_____

_____

_____

_____

_____

_____

_____

Write the rest of the story!

Today was the big day! We put on our costumes and marched right into the president's office. He knew we meant business and that we wouldn't back down without a fight. He spotted us and began laughing manically. He wasn't himself AT ALL. He'd been infected . . .

_____

_____

_____

_____

_____

_____

_____

_____

_____

_____

_____

_____

_____

_____

What's the weirdest thing that has **ever happened** to you?_____

_____

_____.

What's the weirdest thing that you've **ever seen** happen?_____

_____

_____.

Spend an entire day dressed in a costume. Go to the grocery store, run some errands, and visit a bunch of places. Act cool about it. Then write about the experience.

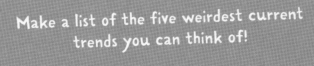

Make a list of the five weirdest current trends you can think of!

1.

2.

3.

4.

5.

Draw something. ANYTHING. Let this page
be your ultimate canvas.

Wouldja change the desktop wallpaper on your friend's computer to something really gross?
YES or **NO**

Wouldja take a gulp of puddle water? **YES** or **NO**

Wouldja whistle and make kissy noises at a cute puppy that walks by you? **YES** or **NO**

Wouldja prank call a local radio station? **YES** or **NO**

Select your favorite and least favorite question from the previous page. Did you respond **YES** or **NO**? Write about your answers and explain why you would (or wouldn't) do the activity.

_____

_____

_____

_____

_____

_____

_____

_____

_____

_____

_____

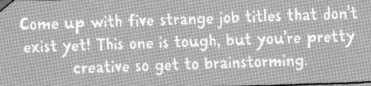
Come up with five strange job titles that don't exist yet! This one is tough, but you're pretty creative so get to brainstorming.

1.

2.

3.

4.

5.

Fill in the blanks.

Fill in each blank with the type of word it requires.
Don't read ahead or think too much. Just do it!

Scott and Jessica walked into the _____
[location]

wearing _____ crowns and holding
[adjective]

very large _____. "We're here to
[plural noun]

_____!" Jessica said. "So grab
[verb]

your _____ and let's go!" Scott
[plural noun]

smiled and began to _____ as
[verb]

the _____ crowd went wild.
[adjective]

Write the rest of the story!

"Make me a grilled cheese sandwich!" a voice shouted from the shadows. We all froze. We knew we were surrounded by one of the deadliest creatures on the planet. And it was hungry. Then everything went black . . .

_____

_____

_____

_____

_____

_____

_____

_____

_____

_____

_____

_____

_____

_____

_____

_____

Draw yourself onto the cover of a **weird fantasy novel**. Become the Elf Captain or Troll Dude you've always dreamed of being.

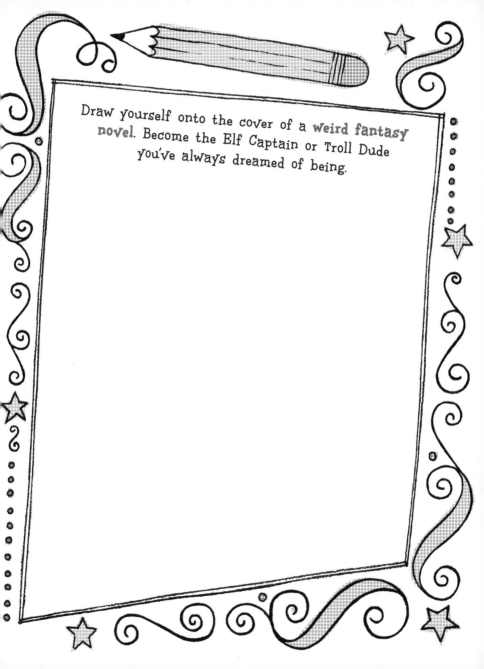

Write the **first thing** that pops into your brain after each word. Don't think about it.

Chirp

_____

Spring

_____

Dough

_____

Living

_____

Slapstick

_____

Dip

_____

Reach

_____

Book

_____

Take a good hard look at your answers on the previous page, and really **THINK** about them. Do you know why you wrote down the words that you did? Figure out your thought process, and try to justify some of your responses.

Fill in the blanks.

Fill in each blank with the type of word it requires. Don't read ahead or think too much. Just do it!

"_____!!! Get your _____
    [plural noun]   [plural noun]

here!" the man shouted. The park was filled with

so many _____ people. You had to
           [adjective]

_____ just to get a seat. I saw a/an
    [verb]

_____with _____ hair
  [animal]   [adjective]

do a funny dance. It was awesome. What a great day.

What if you found out you have an evil twin? Would you seek them out immediately, or would you write them a letter first to feel things out? Write about what you would do.

_____

_____

_____

_____

_____

_____

_____

_____

_____

_____

_____

_____

_____

_____

_____

_____

_____

_____

_____

How do you make a sandwich? Do you throw a bunch of stuff in a pile and then shove it in your mouth, OR do you carefully make a masterpiece? Draw your process in four easy steps!

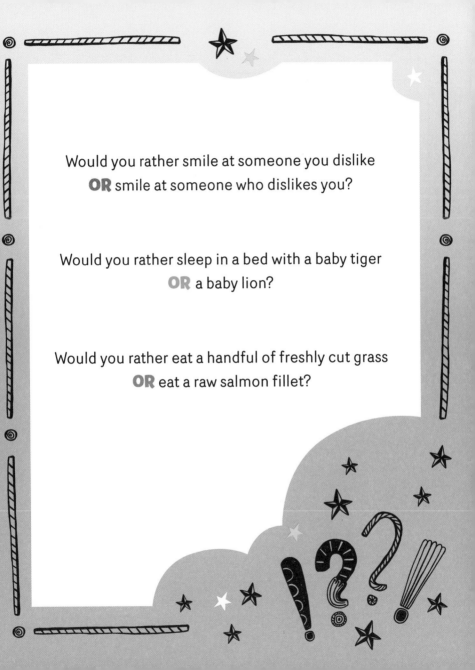

Would you rather smile at someone you dislike **OR** smile at someone who dislikes you?

Would you rather sleep in a bed with a baby tiger **OR** a baby lion?

Would you rather eat a handful of freshly cut grass **OR** eat a raw salmon fillet?

What are five very real fears that someone might have?

1.

2.

3.

4.

5.

Invent five hilarious and weird fears! Nothing scary this time, just funny. Are people afraid of halfhearted smiles? That's just one idea. You don't have to use it if you don't want to.

1.

2.

3.

4.

5.

Write the rest of the story!

Gretel stuck her hand into the cage, giggling. "Come say hello to my pet!" she said. A long snakelike tongue wrapped itself around her arm. "This is Mr. Winkles!" . . .

_____

_____

_____

_____

_____

_____

_____

_____

_____

_____

_____

_____

_____

_____

_____

_____

_____

_____

Draw a **funny logo** for yourself. Does it involve your initials? Is it shaped like a pizza? Get creative!

BOO! Scared you, huh? Now it's your turn. Make up a funny ghost story that'll scare the buhjeebers out of everyone except maybe your grandma. She's got that heart thing.

_____

_____

_____

_____

_____

_____

_____

_____

_____

_____

_____

_____

_____

_____

_____

_____

_____

_____

Imagine it was against the law to eat fruit before noon or wear shorts on the first of the month. INSANITY. Create your own fake laws, and make them as silly as possible!

_____

_____

_____

_____

_____

_____

_____

_____

_____

_____

_____

_____

_____

_____

_____

_____

_____

_____

_____

_____

_____

Being a stand-up comedian looks **fun**, right? But comedians don't just get up on stage and **wing it**. They write their stuff down. On these two pages, try coming up with ideas for a stand-up act.

_____

_____

_____

_____

_____

_____

_____

_____

_____

_____

_____

Test out your act on your friends and family!

Have you ever met someone who you thought was
THE FUNNIEST PERSON EVER, but then you never saw
them again? Bummer. Write about it here.

Draw a naughty T-shirt design!
Nothing scandalous, just something funny
that'll make your mom roll her eyes.

Write the rest of the story!

Doctor Fartknocker turned to the nurse. There was a tear in his eye. Was he crying or laughing? No one could tell until he uttered those three little words . . .

_____

_____

_____

_____

_____

_____

_____

_____

_____

_____

_____

_____

_____

_____

_____

Fill in the blanks.

Fill in each blank with the type of word it requires.
Don't read ahead or think too much. Just do it!

"The _____ is here!" the boy
[noun]

shouted. We'd been watching the sky all night

looking for _____ things, and now
[adjective]

we had one. I tried to _____ it
[verb]

with my _____ but that wasn't
[noun]

happening. "Hurry before it leaves!" said the

boy. I tried using a/an _____
[noun]

but it was too _____.
[adjective]

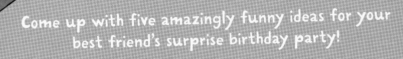

Come up with five amazingly funny ideas for your best friend's surprise birthday party!

1.

2.

3.

4.

5.

Create a list of five silly surprises
you'd like to get on YOUR birthday!

1.

2.

3.

4.

5.

Write the **first thing** that pops into your brain after each word. Don't think about it.

Hashtag

_____

Mad

_____

Shade

_____

Priceless

_____

Jerky

_____

Emo

_____

Title

_____

Ball

_____

Take a good hard look at your answers on the previous page, and really **THINK** about them. Do you know why you wrote down the words that you did? Figure out your thought process, and try to justify some of your responses.

_____

_____

_____

_____

_____

_____

_____

_____

_____

_____

_____

How do you catch a fly? Draw the process in four easy steps.
Well, maybe not EASY. It depends on how quick you are.
Oh, just do it already!

Nursery rhymes are actually pretty crazy and tragic. Make a funny one, why don't you? Lighten up the mood around here.

_____

_____

_____

_____

_____

_____

_____

_____

_____

_____

_____

_____

_____

Write the rest of the story!

"We're trapped," she said, looking out across the vastness of space. "There's no way this ship is getting us home. Not with that THING on board. It smells. You know what we have to do . . ."

_____

_____

_____

_____

_____

_____

_____

_____

_____

_____

_____

_____

_____

_____

_____

_____

_____

What's your **spirit animal**? Draw it below.

What is the funniest piece of clothing that **you own**?

_____

_____

_____

What is the funniest piece of clothing that **someone in your family** owns? _____

_____

_____

What is a funny piece of clothing that you **wish** you owned?_____

_____

_____

Remember when you wrote down the most awkward question you'd never want to be asked? You were just a wee baby back then. Well, it's time to answer it! You're a big kid now.

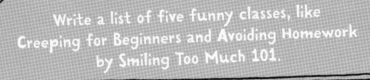

Write a list of five funny classes, like
Creeping for Beginners and Avoiding Homework
by Smiling Too Much 101.

1.

2.

3.

4.

5.

Truth or Dare? That game is old news. **TOTAL FIB** is where someone asks you a Truth question and you answer it. Here's the catch: the person has to decide if it's a real answer or a **TOTAL FIB**. It's a lot funnier if it's a total fib. Play a round with friends, and then write about the experience.

Embarrassing bathroom incidents. **EVERYONE** has had one.
Share one here. Did you get trapped in a Porta-Potty one time?
Shhhh. **No one will tell!**

A lot of funny viral videos are totally setups! (Like the one where that kid picks up a bat and swings it near someone's you-know-what.) What would **YOUR** funny viral video be like?

Write the **first thing** that pops into your brain after each word. Don't think about it.

Dope

Freedom

Space

Clothes

Fly

Alive

Star

Union

Take a good hard look at your answers on the previous page, and really **THINK** about them. Do you know why you wrote down the words that you did? Figure out your thought process, and try to justify some of your responses.

_____

_____

_____

_____

_____

_____

_____

_____

_____

_____

_____

Pretend you were raised by a pack of wolves in the woods. What would be the first paragraph of your autobiography? Write it, and make it extra enticing so we read the rest of the book!

_____

_____

_____

_____

_____

_____

_____

_____

_____

_____

_____

_____

_____

_____

_____

_____

_____

_____

_____

Fill in the blanks.

Fill in each blank with the type of word it requires.
Don't read ahead or think too much. Just do it!

Eliza carefully selected a/an _____
[noun]

from the _____ old cabinet. "This'll
[adjective]

do," she said. "Now I can _____ all I
[verb]

want without those _____ getting
[plural noun]

in my way!" She raised the _____
[adjective]

_____ in the air but quickly
[noun]

got sleepy and went to bed instead.

It's time for your pet lizard's birthday blowout. You'll need to put together a guest list and fun party activities. Don't forget to tell the baker what you'd like the cake to say. Get to it!

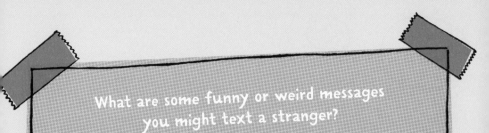

What are some funny or weird messages you might text a stranger?

1.

2.

3.

4.

5.

Write the **first thing** that pops into your brain after each word. Don't think about it.

Water

Transform

Lose

Card

Squad

Chores

Speaker

Tolerate

Take a good hard look at your answers on the previous page, and really **THINK** about them. Do you know why you wrote down the words that you did? Figure out your thought process, and try to justify some of your responses.

Fill in the blanks.

Fill in each blank with the type of word it requires.
Don't read ahead or think too much. Just do it!

The _____ hag reached into her
        [adjective]

sack and pulled out a/an _____.
                                     [noun]

She threw it into the water as it boiled like

a/an _____ in a/an
          [noun]

_____. The villagers began to
  [location]

_____. _____ fell
   [verb]   [plural noun]

from the sky. The spell was finally complete.

What if you could have a brain transplant with **ANYONE** and still retain your own memories and feelings? Who would you choose and why? Write about your reasoning.

_____

_____

_____

_____

_____

_____

_____

_____

_____

_____

_____

_____

_____

How do you spy on a dog? Do you set up a secret camera to watch it from a command center? Maybe you dress up as a different dog? Show us in four panels, spy person.

What are your top five favorite funny Web series?

1.

2.

3.

4.

5.

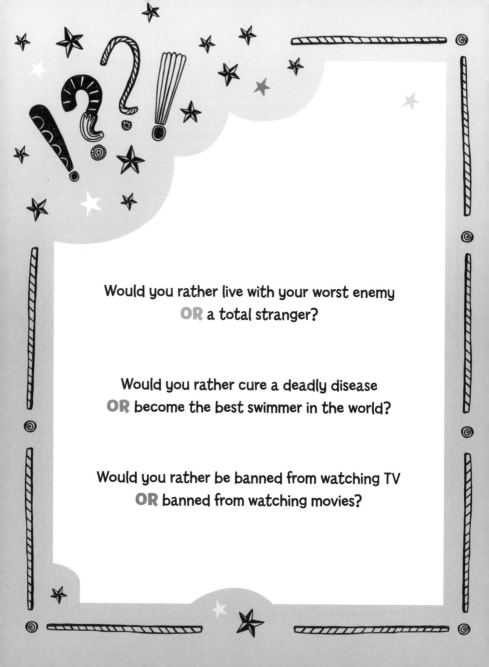

Would you rather live with your worst enemy
OR a total stranger?

Would you rather cure a deadly disease
OR become the best swimmer in the world?

Would you rather be banned from watching TV
OR banned from watching movies?

Draw the world's most **disgusting** food item.
Make sure NO ONE would EVER eat it.

Write the **first thing** that pops into your brain after each word.
Don't think about it.

Hot dog
_____

Treat
_____

Togetherness
_____

Zombie
_____

Forever
_____

Dove
_____

Injury
_____

Tissue
_____

Take a good hard look at your answers on the previous page, and really **THINK** about them. Do you know why you wrote down the words that you did? Figure out your thought process, and try to justify some of your responses.

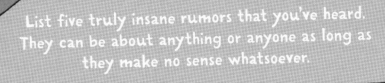

List five truly insane rumors that you've heard.
They can be about anything or anyone as long as
they make no sense whatsoever.

1.

2.

3.

4.

5.

What's a word that always makes you laugh
when you hear it?

What's the funniest sound that you can
think of that's NOT a fart?

What image makes you laugh the most as soon
as you think about it?

Who are your top five funniest TV or Web series hosts?

1.

2.

3.

4.

5.

Who are the top five funniest people you know? If you don't have an Uncle Sal who makes fart noises with his underarm, you can just make them up.

1.

2.

3.

4.

5.

Find a photo of yourself that's NOT your favorite, and then draw a **brand-new version** of it that you LOVE in the space below.

Have you ever said something that YOU thought was hysterical but that other people didn't think was funny AT ALL? Write about that experience.

_____

_____

_____

_____

_____

_____

_____

_____

_____

_____

_____

_____

_____

_____

_____

_____

_____

_____

_____

Cooking is easy, right? I guess you'll see. Come up with a totally new (and kind of wonky) recipe. What **ingredients** are in your dish? What's it called? Have some fun with it.

What are your top five favorite funny quotes
from TV or movies? Make sure to mention who said
it and what it's from!

1.

2.

3.

4.

5.

Go to a grocery store, and select an **exotic** piece of fruit. Draw it below, and give it a weird human face.

Invent a crazy new vacation destination where the beach is weird and the people are giggly. Give it a name, exotic location, and some funny local tourist attractions that'll leave people laughing.

_____

_____

_____

_____

_____

_____

_____

_____

_____

_____

_____

_____

_____

_____

_____

What makes you feel funny? Not the "nauseous like you're going to puke" kind of funny but rather what puts you in a joking mood? Take your time, think hard, and then write about it.

_____

_____

_____

_____

_____

_____

_____

_____

_____

_____

_____

_____

_____

_____

_____

_____

What are five funny questions you might ask someone on a first date? They can be as crazy as you want them to be but you might not get a second date out of it. Aw, who cares? Have a little fun.

1.

2.

3.

4.

5.

What's a strange sport that you've **heard** about?

What's a strange sport that you **wish**
you knew how to play?

What's a strange sport that doesn't **exist** yet?

Who are your top five favorite stand-up comedians?

1.

2.

3.

4.

5.

Who are your top five comedy **LEGENDS**?
If you're not sure, do some research!

1.

2.

3.

4.

5.

You're famous! Come up with three crazy
newspaper headlines about yourself.

And now for today's feature film . . .
THE HILARIOUS STORY OF YOUR LIFE! All that's left is
to give it a title. **Brainstorm** a bunch of good ones.
Get 'em out of your system.

Choose the best title from the ones you just created, and draw up a rollicking movie poster to go with it. Make it GOOD.

What's the funniest gift that you've ever **gotten**?

What's the funniest gift that you've ever **given someone**?

What's the funniest gift that you want but would **never buy** for yourself?

Everyone has at least one item of weird clothing. Use that piece to create the tackiest outfit EVER. Wear it to school one day, and then write about people's reactions.

Get ready because you're creating a **SCAVENGER HUNT**.
Awww yeah. Create a list of six to eight items, and then gather
your friends into small groups. Set a time limit, and send them
off to find everything. Use this space to plan!

Sooo . . . how did the scavenger hunt go? Write about the experience here.

_____

_____

_____

_____

_____

_____

_____

_____

_____

_____

_____

_____

Would you rather drink from a toilet
OR drink from a dog bowl?

Would you rather eat a cricket **OR** eat a spider?

Would you rather tickle someone **OR** get tickled?

Fill in the blanks.

Fill in each blank with the type of word it requires.
Don't read ahead or think too much. Just do it!

The King of _____ entered the
                [plural noun]

castle, noticing a/an _____
                        [adjective]

aroma coming from the kitchen.

_____ for dinner again? The
      [animal]

king wanted something else instead. He

called the town _____, had
                    [job title]

one million _____ delivered
                [plural food item]

immediately, and ate them all in one sitting.

How do you greet a woodland elf? Is it with a smile or a nod? Those little guys sure are cute. Use the four panels below to illustrate your tutorial.

Did you know you're actually royalty? **YOU ARE!** Now create a clever backstory about your secret life as a queen (or king . . . it's all good). **RULING RULES!**

Write the **first thing** that pops into your brain after each word. Don't think about it.

Chicken

_____

Lost

_____

Boy

_____

Gum

_____

Vine

_____

Show

_____

Depressed

_____

Trick

_____

Take a good hard look at your answers on the previous page, and really **THINK** about them. Do you know why you wrote down the words that you did? Figure out your thought process, and try to justify some of your responses.

_____

_____

_____

_____

_____

_____

_____

_____

_____

_____

_____

_____

Wouldja show up to school covered in chocolate, telling people it was "a long night"? **YES** or **NO**

Wouldja go camping in a parking lot? **YES** or **NO**

Wouldja ever make weird faces into a security camera? **YES** or **NO**

Wouldja do a crazy dance in a public place to make your best friend laugh? **YES** or **NO**

Select your favorite and least favorite question from the previous page. Did you respond **YES** or **NO**? Write about your answers and explain why you would (or wouldn't) do the activity.

_____

_____

_____

_____

_____

_____

_____

_____

_____

_____

Write a funny letter to Santa asking for all kinds of crazy stuff. Demand that he gives you the presents you want! Show that bearded weirdo that you mean business.

Grab some flashy clothes and sunglasses, and then head to the mall with your friends. Pretend that you're famous by having your friends run over and ask for your autograph. Write about it below.

_____

_____

_____

_____

_____

_____

_____

_____

_____

_____

_____

_____

_____

_____

_____

_____

_____

Write the **first thing** that pops into your brain after each word.
Don't think about it.

Acceptance

_____

Thirsty

_____

Exotic

_____

Design

_____

Brave

_____

Dead

_____

Menu

_____

Viral

_____

Take a good hard look at your answers on the previous page, and really **THINK** about them. Do you know why you wrote down the words that you did? Figure out your thought process, and try to justify some of your responses.

_____

_____

_____

_____

_____

_____

_____

_____

_____

_____

_____

_____

Draw a crazy **voodoo doll** of yourself!
Does it have straw hair? Does it look deranged?
These are very important questions.

Usually funerals are pretty sad but not today. You're going to write the funniest eulogy EVER. Who kicked the bucket? Doesn't matter. Just leave everyone dying with laughter (pun intended).

Draw the ULTIMATE FORT. This is your **dream fort**.
Is it a treehouse? Is it a luxury condo in Florida?
It's a lot to think about, but you'll be fine.

Write the top five features of the **COOLEST FORT EVER!** Does it have a talking hot tub? **IT SHOULD.**

1.

2.

3.

4.

5.

YOU'VE got the next great idea. Bet you didn't know that, huh? Invent a **crazy new product** that people are sure to love. What does it do? Does it have wacky packaging? Draw it below.

Draw a bunch of laughing smiley faces.
Don't ask why. JUST DO IT!

Fill in the blanks.

Fill in each blank with the type of word it requires.
Don't read ahead or think too much. Just do it!

I finally finished the _____! I had

[noun]

a/an _____ time doing it even though

[adjective]

it made me feel like a/an _____

[food item]

that had been left in a/an _____

[location]

and covered in _____. I had

[noun]

to _____ a lot but it was still

[verb]

fun. I can't wait to _____

[verb]

those _____ again soon!

[plural noun]